A

VIOLIN

—FOR YOUR—

CROW

Acknowledgement

To the one that has lived and died with me on more than one occasion.
Until we meet again in a place even more exhilarating and splendid than this.
Each breath taken is one less closer. Each day lost is one never found.
I will love, embellish and cherish you until the end of time.

"From the Heart comes our love.

From the Soul comes our Humanity.

From the Mind come our Existence.

And to forget any of these things throughout our journey is to create paths of turmoil that twist and turn away from an ending that begets a beautiful Life."

—JWB

Contents

From the Heart

Let It Rain

My head floats
in clouds
tap dancing rainbows
on my brows.
Dew drops of light
dazzle in my dimples
after your love rains
so simple.
So why is the universe
trying to hand me
an umbrella?

Scare Me

Your love scares me.
It creeps inside my head
and creaks when it walks
along the baseboards of my thoughts.
Sometimes it crawls
on the ceiling of my mind
hanging unkind.
Swinging on my impulses
and landing quietly
on my senses.
Sliding down my spine
tickling towards my heart
and before I can look
it disappears.
I can't wait to be frightened
by you again.

Turn Tables

Life is a sphere spinning inside a sphere spinning around a super star.

I imagine sometimes I can reach out and grab the handlebars of its beam and ride a wheelie all the way to heaven!

But it gets dizzy down here sometimes.

Because this merry go round can go round too fast when your heart gets big enough to buy a discounted ticket, but ends up with a very expensive ride all day skip the lines of amusement park life lessons pass.

While your mind impatiently waits single file in anticipation to get on the same thrill that has your heart racing.

So they never seem to be able to get on at the same time and enjoy this ride.

Your heart and your mind don't mind being behind your heart sometimes if it would just settle down, reach back and grab what's under your hat and say "let's do this together because that's better than better, that's forever baby!"

But instead your head can't get ahead cause your heart can't play that part.

So your mind just stands in line while your heart slowly falls apart, quickly as you become sickly from spinning round and round sometimes up most times down, never in a round about way but straight forward.

I say stop wondering how and start wondering now how the great hands that inevitably spin that dial were too large for us to ever dial from the beginning.

So the beginning was your ending.

And if your ending is your beginning, then your beginning was never depending on what Adam and Eve ate in the first place.

That was the worse case scenario for them two dummies to ever be in.

And I'm not agreeing with the picture that I'm seeing.

Nor am I fleeing from the music that be in

my head, spinning round and round on a merry go round, where my heart and my mind never found time to settle down and unwind at the same time.

Because life is a sphere, spinning inside of fear, spinning around a Superstar.

So who do you think you are?

I know who I am.

I am that I am.

And if I am that I am then I am more than I am which means you too are more than you are.

But you can't see that far because you're spinning round and round on a merry go round of ups and downs and clowns that distract you from Life's purpose. And while you watch their circus your purpose can't rise to surface.

So your life that was once priceless is now worthless on purpose.

And whatever now your life's work is, it's worth less than whatever nothing plus nothing minus nothing equals inside of an empty purse.

It's less than worthless!

So let's just have our hearts stand with our minds and patiently wait in line until it's our time to shine like a super star, with our Superstar.

By far that's who we truly are.

As we spin round and round on a merry go round of Life's turn tables!

Feathers in the Wind

Will I ever get tired of chasing feathers in the wind?
You keep on blowing past.
I keep on slowing fast.
And when everything is still,
and silent I will
believe once again
I can catch you.

Two Eggshells

You're the eggshells that I'm walking on.
That's why I tip toe under
standing next to your
understanding
you is like
understanding
me.
I've always misunderstood
us like mist
under stood dust.
I'm the eggshells that you're walking on.
But you're a runner
waiting to plunder
over standing.
And I'm over standing around
waiting for my cracks to ground.
Let's just stay still for awhile
and enjoy us.

Close the Window

Last night my dreams wouldn't dream
I tried to find you leaning against the wall
In a smokey hallway
Traces of lint hugging your hips
In the moonlight pouncing through
That window you left open when you left

Not Now, Later

I don't want to marry you
before I carry you
over all the dangerous
thresholds that you can't see
because you're holding
on to me
with your eyes closed.

A Violin for Your Crow

Later was supposed to come
with angels playing harps
and violins
But your heart's not listening
out for them
It's throwing out breadcrumbs
to crows
and ravens
But they're impatiently waiting
for some real meat.
Here I am.

Deal? Deal!

I'll stop loving you when fish drown.
When trumpets sound, maybe
Say we, not me.
Say us, not thee.
I'll stop loving you where ground floats.
Where nothing hopes
Say we, not me.
Say us, not thee.
I'll stop loving you when courage flees.
When rocks are trees, maybe
Say we, not me.
Say us, not thee.
I'll stop loving you where eagles run.
Where people are none
Say we, not me.
Say us, not thee.
Ok fine...I'll stop when you stop.
Deal?
Deal!

By the Love of You

By the love of you I am blessed and cursed.
You are of a long line of elegance and beauty
as I am from the bowels of the beast himself,
dressed in a knight's splendor with a nobleman's tongue.
Does your ears even welcome me?
Can you feel the light heat of my breath
that is cooled by your presence?
The boldness of your eyes
can calm my weary soul like
that of a mother holding a newborn child.
Oh how your existence holds me!
And while I am stricken by you,
I am in fear but not afraid.
I am confused but enlightened.
And I am overwhelmed but overjoyed.
As you are unaware that in the depths of my heart
your spirit floats high above any and all things,
stationed or vacant in a luminous gown of purity
replacing the moon and causing the waves of my treacherous blood
to burst through a chest that's never been open before.
You are a death goddess that could bring me life.
Close my wombs and teach me
a love that has always beseeched me.
Or the love of you could tighten its hands
around the throat of my sake and close a pinhole
too small for me to live.
As even now I can barely breathe.
And in that I live and die by the love of you.

Waterboard Your Love

You are everywhere life inhales leaving me waiting to exhale into a paper bag full of your playful banter. I'm suffocating on our happiness gasping for another evening of lying next to you while you waterboard me with buckets of passion. Empty them out on me because I'm not caving!

Wilderness Us Two

During the day my love
for you is
swan diving off of splinted tree stumps
into crispy springs,
under waterfalls of a beating heart
running in between rocks of happiness.
During the night my love
for you is
settling down next to small flickers of
camp fire flames,
smoldering over marshmallows dripping
onto tongues of joy while crickets laugh.
As time flies by I hope they don't tire.

Love is definitely blind because you
can't see that I love you.

Love's Scale

It's not always about what you can get or what I can give.
It's not always about when you can leave or when I can stay.
It's not always about where you can go or where I can be.
But it is always about us.
And the weight of all of this makes pounds of difference.

Every Day Should Be

You should be missed every day.
You should be kissed every day.
You should be hugged every day.
You should be loved every day.
And I hope to be lucky enough to see it happen every day.

Is time holding your hand hesitantly like it holds mine? Like it knows I know we don't have time?

Like it knows I know that you're not mine? I could never have something so beautiful because something so beautiful has never had me. Until time started holding mine. Now I'm holding time because time's holding you and between us two time doesn't have time. So is it our time or what?

Haunted Hearts

My heart tried not to be a ghost with you.
It tried to not drown that night when you found yourself
and forgot me.
But it swallowed too much of you.
And I couldn't breathe
as my lungs filled up with regret and
hopes of reconciliation.
Now I'm floating down dark hallways bothering
the good folks that live inside my head.

Adrenaline

I can't wait for you to look up to see me gazing at you.
The rush of us is intoxicating.
You're gushing out of my thoughts.
My head can't hold the memories of your love.
My body's shaking as your presence consumes me.
Come here so I can bite you and taste you one last time.
And another last time.
And another.
And.

My Love for You Reigns True

I'll never tire.
It's more than desire.
A million miles walked each step resembles a stride.
An infinity of travel worth my feelings inside.
Though they can be buried, they cannot be ignored.
Love is the unknown that must be explored.
And once it's uncovered the truth blinds bright
that no matter the time of day or of night,
my love for you
reigns true.

Questions Never Answered

Even though the distance
between us is as long as the Nile,
it empties into the Mediterranean
of my patience and inability
to dry myself out of your hold on me.
So my love for you flows into
your love for me
watering the sands of your
heart as you soak up my
time and energy.
The only question is
should I trickle into more
accepting terrain willing to be
nourished by my love?
Well, does a river get to
pick its own path?
Or does it flow where
the wind and rocks of existence
push it?

The Refugee in Me

I can give you everything
and still you feel as if you have nothing.
I can give you nothing
and yet you feel that you have everything.
Your love is as fickle as a whisper
inside of a whirlwind.
I can never make out what's being said.
I can only see my feelings
being dropped from the top of your funnel.
And the aftermath of damage
that remains when your storm ends.
So why do I take cover
in the eye of your storm
or cold heartedly seek refuge
away from the blazing sun?
You tell me.

Our love is magnetic so me being North and you being South works.
It's when you're trying to be North that you push me away.
So southern up already!

Dirty Money

I would suggest
a penny
for your thoughts
of me
loving you but
then I'd be
unethically
rich.

Feed Our Fire

This flame can't be blown out by disbelief.
It deserves you blowing on it as much as I.
And when the light starts to flicker in the middle of the night
I can't be the only one of us two willing to die
breathing life back into it.
Your lungs are a lot stronger than mine.
I've been blowing for a long time.
And our love is waiting for you to feed it now.
In the middle of the storm I'm wondering how
you don't realize we need this flame
to make it through.

All Things Are Nothing

I see your face in clouds sometimes,
softening the majestic glow of the sun.
I see your reflection in noonday puddles
rippling under quiet breezes.
I see your personality
piercing through thorn bushes
a blossoming red enlightening
the scenery.
I see you in everything that is anything
and anything that means everything.
And all things are are nothing
until they are you.

Love Games

I would play games with our love
like rolling dice and pouncing props
around the board of us,
but the playing pieces would eventually
slide off the edge,
crash to the floor
and roll under an old emotional sofa
never to be found again.
I would play games with our love
like shuffling random cards
and passing them out with fingers crossed
hoping to best the opposing side
of self doubt and insecurity
only to be dealt an entourage of losing cards.
I would play games with our love
like pushing the joystick anxiously
left and right, up and down
pressing buttons aggressively until
ultimately the console screen of reality
says game over.
I would play games with our love
but I just don't play games when it comes to our love.

I would die to live with you as I live to die with you.
So all I ask of you is to live and die with us.

Don't Leave

My love for you trickles
down my cheek sometimes.
It drips into memories of you
splashing happiness on my face.
It's cold outside
but warm and cozy in here.
Won't you beg the powers to let you stay
a little while longer than yesterday?
Because today you're tomorrow's anticipation
as I knew you would be!

Crumb Cake Crackle Puffs

I'd like to have a bowl please.
Waking up to dimples spread across smiling cheeks
in between last night's pleasantries
and this morning's kisses I'd
make a home.
Add sugar and milk to mine please.
With a glass of sunshine on the side I'd
stay forever.

I Love Your Beautiful Mind

I'm in love with the way you think.
Johnnie Walker, I'm in love with the way you drink.
Our love is Zelda, legendary,
I'm in love with the way you Link.

Cool Love

Can I be cool with you?
Can I listen to the moon with you?
Can I tip toe the stars around your heart?
What I love about us is
most people don't get to fall in love like this.
But it's so cool.
Can I be cool with you?
Can I makes some cool moves with you?
Can I break some rules with you.
It's up to you to take us
somewhere we can love until it's cool.
Because it's so cool.
Cool love.

Poppy in a Red Dress

Meet me in the poppy fields of love
barefoot in your red dress and finesse
the worms beneath your feet.
I'll be there looking from the stars
begging father to allow me back down
for a visit.
I'll be the wind feathering your thighs.
I'll be the stardust tickling your eyes.
Cry for me.

Crimson Sky

There's a crimson sky because of you tonight.
The moon bled when you fled.
There's a chill in our bed.
And there will be no sleep because of it.
Let the horizon crash upon my head oh God
so I can forever rest too.
Let the clouds swallow me up
that parted for you.
Or they can vomit you up
and give you back to me.
Let it be oh God or let me be.
For there's a crimson sky because of you tonight.

Catch Me If I Fall

Your love is blinding.
Shining so bright that I can't see where I'm going.
If my foot dashes against the edge of fear
will you drop your wall and catch me?

So I Climb

Snow's falling
On my head
While I climb
The air is getting thin
While I climb
Pebbles rustle down
While I climb
The wind cuts so deep
While I climb
I know your love awaits me at the top
So I climb
So I climb
So I climb
So I climb
So I climb
So I climb
So I climb
So I climb
So I climb
So I climb
So I climb
So I climb
So I climb
So I climb
So I climb
So I climb
So I climb
So I climb
So I climb
So I climb
So I climb
So I climb
So I climb

So I climb
So I climb
So I climb
So I climb
So I climb
So I climb
So I climb
So I climb
So I climb
So I climb
So I climb
Then I fell
So I climb

Dandelion Lover

Your love is a dandelion
Blowing on my face
I can feel the wind
As it barely beats you
Softly against my skin
Up my nose
Making me sneeze
Making me laugh
Making me love

Butterfly Lies

Caterpillars turn into butterflies
like the cocoon of lies you told me
fly off in my mind,
except not as pretty.

You walked off the edge of a great cliff and plunged into an ocean of unforgiveness.
I saw you.
I dived to the bottom through sea monsters to find you.
I found you.
I pulled you out and lay you on solid ground.
You died.
I breathed into your lungs and pumped your stomach.
You gagged.
You spit up persecution strangled by depression.
I smiled.
Now you live again.
And so do I.
I walked off the edge of a great cliff and plunged into an ocean of unforgiveness.
You saw me.
But the monsters in the sea scared you.
So you left.
I died.

I love the smell of you.

Not the perfume or cologne sleeping on your skin.

But the smell of you hugging me good morning.

I love the smell of happiness on the tip of your tongue when you tell me secrets.

Or the smell of togetherness when we're holding hands.

Smells like forever.

Closed Eyes Breathing

When they shut my heart pumps harder
reminding me when my best life was.
They keep rolling back as memories roll forward.
Rolling, rolling and rolling some more.
Happy, healthy and hurting no more
until they open back up again.
I'm breathing best when they're closed.
I hold my breath and exhale when they're closed again
because when they're not the memories are not the same.
Every time I awake it's way too soon!

What if we could stay down here forever?
Underneath all odds of the inevitable disappointment
of being disappointed
lies the truth of you and I.
We'd sleep together instead of being awake alone
dreaming of swing dancing with each other's destinies.
I'd dip you over a pool of glee of you and me
while looking deep into the windows of your thoughts.
Kiss me now while we're still down here.
Hold me until we're dragged back to surface
and once we're there try not to forget who we were
just moments before the ascend.

I would have followed you to the moon but you wouldn't move. So I picked you up and carried you there. I left to pick the sun out of the sky for you, but when I returned you had run off to catch some shooting stars and got lost in my shadow. I'll never find you unless I lose the sun and losing myself is not an option because the last time I did that, the universe went pitch black. So I'll hold onto me until you find the moon I first placed you on. Until then, I love you!

Watch Them Burn Out With Me

The eagle comes back to the nest after babies awake from their rest.
Like bees come back to the hive and ants to the sugar cube.
Return to the mood we once had.
With outstretched arms I'd receive the warmth you once gave.
Both lives of ours we'll save
and rave about past laughs and giggles.
Your love wiggles under a blanket of woven warm emotions.
I'd swim through stormy oceans to beach with you
or reach with you heights unknown.
The lights alone that hang from the sky
would eventually dull in due time without you
watching them burn out with me.
So as long as it takes just watch them burn out with me.

Don't Want To

The teacher smacked my hands with a ruler for not doing so.
And it seems pretty selfish of me.
I'm trying to be a better person.
I'm looking to grow.
And I want to improve.
But I just don't want to share you with anyone else.
It should be fine because you're not crayons anyway.

Your Love is Instrumental

Like pushing on weighted piano keys
it takes some effort to make a wondrous sound
pressing on your heart.
But once pushed down upon
can pronounce beautiful
harmonious melodies
that the entire world should hear.
It would be my pleasure to sing
along with your beating heart.
But my voice is not worthy enough
to tip toe across the same waves.
Though I'd give you
a violin for your crow
I don't believe I could carry the burden.
Nor would you allow it.
But I thought I'd ask anyway.
Because the sound of losing you
is all the instruments imaginable
playing off notes all at once.

Love's Scale

It's not always about what you can get or what I can give.
It's not always about when you can leave or when I can stay.
It's not always about where you can go or where I can be.
But it is always about us.
And the weight of that is what makes us different.

Misunderstood

My reflection gets tampered in a wave
of emotion.
I need you to be smart enough to save
me and I'm hoping
that it's true that it's you
who's paddling to save me.
Who's paddling to save me?
Cause I'm drowning in the shallow end of being misunderstood.
My soul gets trampled, centipedes
they're running over
with the weight of the world killing me
on my shoulders.
Is it true that it's you
who's battling to save me?
Who's battling to save me?
Cause I'm dying when the battle ends of being misunderstood.

From the Soul

Safe Travels

To go against me is to surprise your own reflection,
futility at its best, embarrassing to your sub conscious and
mocking the truth you already know.
It's a long walk to paradise
when you run the opposite way and only turn around
because your shadow bested you to hell.
And I know where you've been because the spine of your character reeks of
devilish smoke and feels like fresh ash.
And with outstretched arms in vain I embrace your tainted grace from whence
you've come a long way to be nowhere,
still death and subliminally silent, yet your meaningless words sway to the beat
of my heart and stomp ridiculously loud inside my head.
And I hate the sound they create together a miserable song both demon and
angel instinctively dance.
Until death do we part
now or later.
When you've completed your path and mine dries up
since love started wet with tears of affection
and now sit on a dusty, damp road of uncertainties and
imperfections,
as I still wish you safe travels.

Turn Tables

Life is a sphere,
spinning inside a sphere,
spinning around a super star that I imagine
sometimes I can reach out
and grab the handlebars of its beam
and ride a wheelie all the way to heaven!
But it gets dizzy down here sometimes
because this merry go round can go round too fast
when your heart gets big enough to buy a discounted ticket
but ends up with a very expensive ride all day
skip the lines of amusement park life lessons pass.
While your mind impatiently waits single file in anticipation
to get on the same thrill that has your heart racing.
So they never seem to be able to get on at the same time
and enjoy this ride
your heart and your mind don't mind
being behind your heart sometimes
if it would just settle down,
reach back
and grab what's under your hat
and say "let's do this together because that's better than better that's forever baby!"
But instead your head can't get ahead
cause your heart can't play that part.
So your mind just stands in line while your heart slowly falls apart,
quickly as you become sickly
from spinning round and round
sometimes up, most times down.
Never a round about way but straight forward
I say stop wondering how and start wondering now
how the great hands that inevitably spin that dial
were too large for us to ever dial
from the beginning!

So the beginning was your ending.
And if your ending is your beginning
then your beginning was never depending on what Adam and Eve ate in the
first place.
That was the worse case scenario for them two dummies to ever be in!
And I'm not agreeing with the picture that I'm seeing,
nor am I fleeing from the music
that be in my head.
Spinning round and round on a merry go round
where my heart and my mind never found time to settle down
and unwind at the same time.
Because life is a sphere,
spinning inside of fear,
spinning around a Superstar.
So who do you think you are?
I know who I am!
I am that I am
and if I am that I am
then I am more than I am
which means you too are more than you are.
But you can't see that far
because you're spinning round and round
on a merry go round of ups and downs
and clowns that distract you from Life's purpose.
And while you watch their circus
your purpose can't rise to surface!
So your life that was once priceless
is now worthless on purpose.
And whatever now
your life's work is worth less
than whatever

nothing plus nothing minus nothing
equals
inside of an empty purse
it's less than worthless!
So let's just have our hearts stand with our minds
and patiently wait in line
until it's our time to shine
like a super star with our Superstar.
By far that's who we truly are
as we spin round and round
on a merry go round of Life's turn tables!

Muse

The world is not a muse.
It's a distraction.
But I can't lose if I have a counter reaction.
So I choose to use every inch of it
from horrific news to clues
of indefinite
public racism and humiliations of God's creations.
I rise above the loveless.
Cause men love less than less unless it's of negative interest
that compiles interest or tax deductions.
While the fact is dozens of innocent homeless children
roam this place we call home.
As we call home from behind a jail cell and bars of imprisonment
to loved ones who never envisioned it
would ever be a sea of orange jumpsuits and commissary.
As we carry poverty's cross across the hills of times lost
and recklessly climb up the burning mountainsides of dimes lost.
We end up on top of the repetitive ash of a whole lot of great and powerful
minds lost.
To only tumble all the way down into a valley of mental starvation's holocaust.
But I find hope inside of a note that I once wrote without a note pen.
This note is the same sound that my ancestors found
when chains and whips of insanity
gripped around the necks of humanity
and made mankind reek of desolation and isolation from the revelation of our
destination!
Because this world is not a muse, it's just a distraction
trying to stop me from becoming me,
trying to block me from becoming free,
trying rob me of my destiny but that's less than me!
Stop arresting me and start investing in me.
Stop inspecting me and start expecting me
to be the rising sun that I have become.
So I can shine on you and expose the truth

that she is not a muse, she's just a distraction!
While she tries to bruise your thoughts with stiletto hills
on designer shoes and hot pink mini skirts
while she plots on your mind's demise and your heart's destruction.
Between her thighs lies corruption
and upon her lips lies the excess consumption
of condescending words and contradicting verbs
that regurgitate back up from the pits of hell
of her beautiful belly dancing
and spill back out the side of her twisted mouth as loving advice.
That's just a vice to splice
your Redwood tree of will to succeed,
to secede your blossom of success
back to a seed of hopelessness
and despair.
But you are unaware because you're still amused
and certainly confused by the softness of her lips
and boldness of her hips
that makes you believe that she's still a muse.
But she's not a muse, she's just a distraction!
As your interaction with meaningful actions
slowly become irrelevant actions lacking the passions
to pursue happiness and explore your own greatness.
Instead you receive fakeness
and empty promises around the tainted seams
of an overpriced engagement ring that means absolutely nothing
because it was purchased on the backs of the fact that
he never had intentions of marrying you.
Instead he only had intentions of burying you
beneath the bile ridden soils of your own insecurities and desperations
that inevitably lead to futile investigations
of truths that you can never prove.
But you already know that he's not a muse, he's just a distraction!
All words no action.
It's absurd to only have a fraction
of his heart while his attraction

to the art of self destruction makes your relationship convulsive
and turns you into a compulsive
liar as you try to convince yourself that he truly loves you.
When deep down inside the tombs
of your solemn wrapped soul
you surely understand and know that he can only love himself.
Which defecates your health
and ruins your chances of becoming that beacon in the storm.
I'm speaking out the norm to help you to form
a better view of you.
They never knew of you because you never knew of you.
So it's only up to you to become a better you.
Because it's already too few of us truly trying to do.
So if we're truly trying to do why then is the number truly so few?
Cause if the number was more we could rise from the floor,
walk through the door of oppression
with our heads held high and scream out a battle cry
to wake up this nation of abomination
and persecutions we seem to always be facing.
And bring freedom and equality of life
to everyone and every body that abides this earth
because we all have worth.
And until you realize your own worth upon this earth,
you too are not a muse.
You're just a distraction!

I Just Didn't Believe

It started as a seed that was maliciously planted by greed
and handed down by the blood stained palms
of those whose wrongs have never been right.
But right away your mind gave way like old rotted wood
infested by termites of negativity and despair that continue to
wear down and tear down what's left of your imagination.
Is your mind God's creation or the devil's plantation?
Your lack of motivation and dedication
to greatness was an invented hate list
scribbled by Satanist with crippled fingers of fakeness
on demonic scrolls
wrapped around totem polls
of pain that stretched inside your brain
and made you believe in broken.
And spoken out of their mouths hateful words like
Nigger, Spic, Chink, Hick
all spit to make it hard for you to make it.
While your soul lies naked under hatred,
it was the world that raped it
under the shade of a tall mighty tree
planted by a sea of iniquity that continues to grow
and spread its thorn stricken branches
throughout the bright skies of your lonely heart.
They made you believe in the dark.
As they covered up the view of true you
with shallow thoughts and perverted plots
darkening what was left of that small sprinkle of a twinkle in your eye.
But there is a wrinkle in the sky that you can't deny.
It's a silver line that's waiting for you to tight rope and walk across to freedom.
But they have tainted your mind with poisonous cyanide
to suffocate you into thinking that you can't beat them.
They're choking you with a deceitful grip
while you can't get a grip on the reality that you can be them.
They know what it takes to break you,

but what will it take to wake you
up from this long hibernation
of poverty and hyper evasion
of a higher quality of living.
They tricked you into pimping and drug dealing
instead of dealing with love of such divine healing
from up above that's been rooted in your blood since the beginning of blood.
So your mind floods with mud
from their filthy hands that tie the shoe strings of insecurity
and fear around the feet of your thoughts.
So now your plots can't move and your thoughts can't groove.
They just sit there wasted.
Look at all the time you've wasted!
Sweet dreams you've never tasted
because you've lost the basic will to make it.
They told you that you were less than basic
and treated your head like a vacant
lot to only park dump trucks filled with thoughts
of suicidal garbage.
And in that concrete jungle nothing good can harvest
because your heart has hardened to its hardest.
And when you try to harness
all the strength you can muster
to shake loose from the rusty chains that cluster
as metallic cobwebs of suppression
weighing down and suppressing
every single good thing that's bound inside of you.
They made you believe you were nothing!
By cutting and thrusting
lies on top of lies that they disguise
in hypocritical blockbusters that demolish your third eye
and leave you helplessly blind
roaming place to place without faith
while hope leaves your face and you become an ugly disgrace
to the human race.
As happiness disappears from your race without a trace.

They made you believe you were something
when they tricked you into killing your own brethren
because of the color of a rag
when rags is all we had and the whole world was glad
we had inflicted war upon ourselves.
As our wells run dry and our communities die
from them continually pumping that welfare drug
into the arms of our brain
leaving us dumb and lame unwilling to change
accepting this insane way
to live our day to day.
And in vain we kneel and pray
to our Father to take us further
as we beg him to place us in universities like Harvard or Yale
while their intentions are to keep us educated behind the bars
of a jail cell
when all you've learned
is the proper way to make bail!
You have committed yourself to marrying a prison cell.
But it's well past time to unveil
the hell beneath that veil
she wears and swears by.
Hiding her true intentions to make you feel
comfortable with being behind bars
by feeding you Snicker bars and slices of devil's cream pie
at suppertime to help you slowly die
inside the arms of the law.
And though they've tried to hide these truths
behind their flashy nightclubs and V.I.P. booths,
this is what I always saw.
And the only difference between you and I
is that when they tried to make me believe I
was nothing.
I just didn't believe I was nothing!

Peace Embrace Our Sleep

There are dark corners where games are being played by those who live to see others not.

It is in these times that we must allow our lives to shine so bright that shadows flee and game boards flip over.

This land is too beautiful to be yours or mind.

We cannot possess what we truly admire.

We must aspire to awe and share its magnificent wonder.

And the moment that realization rings true to all is the same moment that peace embraces our sleep.

You Are a Book of Life

We as human beings need to acknowledge the pages of our perception.

We must be consciously aware of the narrative our book of life reads.

And the only way to honestly know how that narrative reads is by reflecting on what others perceive of us.

The story that we think our life is telling everyone is not always on the same page of what is truly being read.

We are all authors of our own legacy and there's excitement in that alone.

But we must remember that the lives we write everyday is being written not for us, but for them. And even though we already know our own story, it is others that may be confused when reading us.

So as human beings we must take responsibility for their confusion as we are the artist of our own life's book.

Therefore our stories are only as good as the reviews rendered.

And as writers we must indulge the needs of our audience if we truly care about those we interact with while the pages of our lives are still being turned.

Let's Trade

I'll give you some lemonheads for your bubble gum.
That's double dumb if you don't like lemon water.
But trade me anyway.
I'll give you my soul for a taste of freedom.
Though you'll never free them so that's ridiculous.
But trade me anyway.
I'll give you poverty to ride this cloud.
However to get in you have to step down.
But trade me anyway.
I'll give you all of me for none of you.
And now you're confused because I am you.
But trade me anyway.
Trade me any way.

Eternal Flame

You didn't deserve anything,
yet the world gave you everything
except humility,
which should have been wrapped inside
a box of passion for humanity.
But instead you got privilege incased in hatred
delivered by blood stained hands.
The sarcasm at the top of your brow and
on the corner of your lips
lights a fire in us that'll burn until it doesn't.

Ahh Haa

Are these bars on the windows to keep
the monsters in or out?
The bus doesn't have a route
I'd like to take
an underground railroad
to me.
But took an over the top highway
to you and your criticism
of everything lovely.
And everything lovely isn't
every thing
so I didn't get anything at all
in this except this.

Unleashed

The power that's within me is no longer within.

It has decided to emerge from beneath the rubble that buries greatness and consumes the best of men.

Slowly it pushed through the bowels of vile imagination grabbing hold of something so true that even the lies of discrimination had to bow down to royal blood pumping furiously through veins of hope feeding oxygen to brains of undoubted existence.

The power is no longer within me but out in the open fields of consciousness running rapid crushing everything under toe with an elephant's weight of earned understanding.

The pound of its feet pivoting against the world's disbelief frightens them, but enlightens me as the Universe steps aside to feel the wind as it whisks by carrying me on its shoulders.

He smiles and nods his head in approval, as he's always known my path holds no boundaries nor stares in any stereotypical direction.

Shame on them that believed in less than the excellence of my execution and the righteousness of my rise over persecution as they are now laying rail that is too frail to support my progress.

I am freer than the dust storms of the mighty rings of Saturn, as the power within is no longer within.

My mind has realigned with me and we have decided to never part ways again. For the power within is no longer within.

I am unleashed!

Statue

Look at how they got you.
See I'm not mad at you for being angry with them.
I'm just sad that you're not the gem you were meant to be.
You were sent to be a jewel in the sun, a miraculous one, a Juliet Rose.
But I suppose you would have rose if planted in golden soil but instead your feet froze in that sinister cold hypocritical old cement they keep casting you in.
Statue!
But I'm not mad at you.
I'm just sad that you keep standing there unaware of where, where is.
There is freedom in your boots but you can't walk that line.
You're running out of time just standing in line waiting for deliverance, that's your hindrance.
Nobody's body is coming, nobody's running, nobody's gunning to shoot down those assassins that's tasked with melting your brain like plastic as they blast it with drastic heat waves of elastic stretched truths and gastric lies.
They each did.
Your teacher did.
Your preacher hid when confronted by the devil.
Instead of being a rebel and grabbing a shovel and burying that great book he took something he couldn't understand and put it in your hand, but not for free.
See you get charged a fee for your soul to be set free, but not me!
How many offerings does it take for your soul to escape the hell they created to elevate themselves to a higher place while you patiently wait for a blessing to regulate your life?
Statue!
But life's already your blessing so stop stressing and start progressing by investing in yourself.
If not you, then who?
Who better than you to know what your strengths truly are?
You're better than whatever polyester sweater of oppression they keep dressing you in.
That's not a sweater it's a straight jacket.
So straight jack it and hack it off your back with an ax of enlightenment.

Don't be frightened, this next thing will sting but you're already stung.

You're trying to hang out with them but you're already hung by devilish songs that's sung by the same slithering tongues that lashed out and spit poverty on you and called it a hymn.

That's not a hymn.

It's just him Hatred disguised beneath high hypnotic tunes and low demonic tones that you confuse as love jones and fall into a trance believing that your mind is enhanced while you holy dance to an alter built to alter your existence. When in fact it only keeps you haltered in the same holster of no resistance to the resistance of you moving ahead while your head is bowed and your eyes are closed and feet still froze in the same spot that you chose not, but was chosen for you before you was you.

Statue!

If the truth could truly set you free how come it's not being sold to you for free? Everything you've been told has been given to you by those who originally hated you, degraded you and bated you into drug addiction, nicotine affliction, tobacco picking, alcoholic slurred words and jail conviction.

Now hell's inscription is being branded in your brain while they make you take out a student loan for every single ambitious thing your feeble mind can entertain.

When everything they claim has been deemed a lie just to make you lie in the same lye that could never wash away the dye of the blood, sweat and tears from years and years of mental slavery that has majorly stunted your growth from the inhaling of deceptive smoke that your mind continues to puff, puff, pass. You're no different than an ass that continues to be whipped on its ass by a master who is inspired by cash while you're inspired by trash like grass and twigs when your hooves are big enough for you to simply turn around, rise up from the ground and stomp your so called master down.

But you still got your head down embellished by ground that your ancestors died for that was promised to be yours but never given.

But how could something be given that's already owned unless it's taken?

But you're too stubborn of an ass to get past your past so you just continue to graze in this concrete jungle of unforgiving grass while your enemy continues to lean on your ass.

Statue!

But I'm not mad at you.

I'm just sad that you continue to dream of things that seem to never lean towards your wellbeing like expensive cars you can't afford and bars when you get bored that swipe your credit card for you to pour that cheap poison through your pores that leaves your vision impaired.

Not your vision to drive from here to there but your vision to rise up to where no one could ever hold you down ever again.

Because you my friend are not a statue!

Just because you fly first class doesn't mean you're first class. Some of the best people I've met fly coach.

The World Is Not Your Friend

The World is not your friend.

It's just your motivation.

And before your time can end you should be looking for a standing ovation, high enough to touch clouds of greatest and loud enough to wake up the subconscious of your peers.

So they too can rise up from the rears and elevate to the front of life's line.

Yesterday was born and already today needs a lifeline.

Tomorrow is not promised to form but if born could be twice blind to the irrationalities of poverty's nationalities, working against each other head to head to get ahead.

When instead the only way to get ahead is to head towards the hills of togetherness and climb hand in hand every woman, every man, every tribe, and every clan needs to backseat their egos in society's caravan and press the pedal to the metal of humanity.

Because the World is not your friend, it's just insanity.

It woke up today and looked into the mirror of forgiveness and only saw vanity.

So your own reflection of yourself is only the perception of those with wealth trying to manipulate your mind with wine squeezed from grapes picked from trees of hate, planted by the same hands that can't wait to slap down your ideas until your dreams are dead.

There are negative streams ahead that you shouldn't drink from, and relative things ahead that you shouldn't become accustomed to.

Because your customs too can be deceiving.

The World and its culture are cousins of manipulation.

Today the media is simply an infection slowly clawing away at your common sense.

Therefore your life has been common since the birth of sister radio and her younger brother television.

They're trying to sell a vision of poisonous propaganda that could have you miss becoming a papa or a grandma because you've died choking on spoiled truths they forced you to swallow.

Now your young seeds are forced to wallow with their heads held down because they can't borrow figs from a treacherous money tree called credit.

That was ultimately designed to discredit anyone whose skin is bronzed without the help of the sun.

No the World is not your friend, it's just your motivation.

And you certainly cannot win without your mentality courageously facing the enemy in the eye and yelling a battle cry stating I will not be denied success.

Because the World is not my friend, it's just my access to assess things as they truly are.

I am temporarily a fallen star just visiting the lies of this planet.

Granted you can't see the worth in me because your eyes can't adjust to the illuminating light that's bouncing off my ideas striking your injustice in the face and casting shadows of truth to shade me from the heat of deceit brewing in your private clubs and bewitched corporate halls.

Everything formed against me shall fall as I begin my ascend, where should I begin?

Should I start where your heart stomped on Vietnam or where you dropped the first Atom Bomb?

Should I start with worldwide genocide on generations that tried to hide from the malice you created all from your sense of entitlement while you invaded the inhabited lands of people who would have gladly embraced you with hands of welcome?

You're welcome for us slaving them railroads and paving your golden streets East to West on the orient express to financial imprisonment.

That's not the picture you cheaply painted or the way we envisioned it.

40 acres and a mule was just a tool used to confuse everyone that had nothing to die for, to pick up a gun and die for something or someone not willing to do the same for them.

What's 40 acres to us who already own everything inside of the equator?

While your feet's in alligator and coach hangs on your shoulder barefoot I cross your borders to build your cities that inject segregation in my veins leaving my kind to only be embarrassed by your needles of arrogance and junky scars of discrimination.

So this World is not my friend, it's just my motivation to continue to rise to the occasion to not be pulverized by orchestrated inflation but to evolve inside of a nation that's leading the world to its own damnation.

I make peace with all past cynical situations and forgive myself for accepting any false interpretations of the truth.

Whether it be delivered by the rich, the poor, the old or the youth.

I will continue to elevate far above the clouds to reclaim my place amongst life's stars.

Encouragingly but earnestly pulling at the arms of my true friends as we all help each other to ascend beyond the points of our own imaginations.

While remembering whole heartedly and emphatically that the World is not our friend as it is only our motivation!

But I'm Not

He reaches for me with outstretched arms like a river spreading itself across the land just for its hands to hug the sea, as if I'm the greatest man to walk the earth. But I'm not.

She smiles at me with tiny teeth, her mouth full of stars and face lit up like a cloudless night sky dancing on God's stage a humbled performance, as if I'm worthy to have front row seats to her loving me.

But I'm not.

She unconditionally follows me into the holes of life's caves blindfolded by a loyal heart tightly tied around her mind cutting into the dreams of her skin and bleeding into her trusting eyes as if I'm the only one that could lead us to freedom. But I'm not.

They believe in me like dessert life waiting for a melancholy heaven to finally sigh and cry some rain just enough for them to not die, but grow just to patiently wait again and again until the next sob as if I'm some messiah honorable enough for them to have faith in.

But I'm not.

I am only a human with a history of faults no different than the earth that quakes as lava erupts from my soul randomly without warning burning my existence in an attempt to simply live a life believed is owed.

But it's not.

As both believers and doubters with eyes wide open watch each animated scene of a show with dimmed lights and smoky disposition believe in some way, shape or form that I will inevitably and ultimately fail at dominating this life.

But I'm not!

Beautiful America

With squinted vision this land was seen beautiful.

While eyes wide shut watched a hated people bite cuticles. Waiting to exhale, a breath yet to be fully taken.

We awaken from choking on stale air.

The Devil's dew that lightly sat upon silver tongues whispered a grievous stench disguised under melodic hymns that seem to still dampen senses.

So we cough up excuses to not listen to reason.

The noises that pound inside our head never silence our sneezes.

Powerful words spoken but never followed are just logs of rotted tear dried wood chopped from trees of hypocrisy burning in empty fireplaces within our stone cold hearts.

We find these truths to be self evident that all men are created equal, but the hands of poverty in America have separated the likeness of all people.

So how beautiful is this America?

Beauty doesn't cry wolf to devour men's souls and leave kindred spirits starving for freedom.

Life spits in our faces because Liberty has been drinking from a vile glass filled with toxic beliefs that it easily swallowed but couldn't hold down.

And Pursuit of Happiness has run dryer than the deserted oasis of our optimism.

That same oasis that allowed America to free itself from a Britain not so great, to eventually partake in the same mistakes.

Is this not insanity?

Or is it that Vanity has put on her clogging boots to river dance all over our common sense?

Stomping on our ambitions to diagnose us with symptoms of headache.

Then feeding us an antidote of hopeless despair pills that swell up inside the bellies of our mind and somehow leave them unimaginatively hollow.

It's cruel and unusual how thirteen colonies not so original birthed colleges like Harvard that took Yale's hand and signed that crooked dotted line not allowing the poor to attend.

So if you were poor you couldn't ascend.

And if your skin was a shade darker than pale then America felt it was her right to make us carry water pales to wells we could never own.

Just to wash our master Democracy's feet and sit helplessly as he walked all over our feeble minds wrinkling our thoughts of promise like a cheap, worn out welcome mat.

While America sent her springs to college we slaved outside her cottage and pick cabbages for her to eat while she put cabbage in her baggage and traveled the world in style we traveled her fields in single file as savages and averaged less than life as she multiply life twice and lived it out to its fullest for the both of us! Beauty is in the eye of the beholder.

But when you're holding everything you can't see how ugly you truly are.

So America is less than beautiful by far!

Independence day is only the anniversary of America still contemplating whether or not to say yes to Democracy when he proposes.

Democracy well aware she'll only marry for greed is promising her the equator for a wedding ring.

But that ring rest round the fingers of thirteen others.

And since America is too rich to share and Democracy is too proud to kneel even to propose, it would seem that us true folk are still waiting for an invitation to a wedding that we'll never be invited to.

So the only ones to end up on bended knee in this country are we!

As the pounds of discrimination weigh all of us down, too heavy a crown for any of our heads to host.

We'll never get to be the queens and kings we're destined to be until the burden of that weight is lifted like the wings of the flight of an eagle.

And that American bird is not her only endangered species!

Is this why we're being held in captivity?

Captivity being the penitentiary where many of us unwarrantedly reside.

A poor child silently cries inside jealous that Jesus' father's house has many mansions while his father's house only has many windowless rooms with iron bars and restricted visiting hours while America cowards behind a constitution with no restitution!

So the only true thing that's beautiful about this America is the beautiful people that live in it that haven't given up on her and Democracy yet.

We Just Think Differently

The difference between you and I is that you are willingly praying to get to an afterlife while they steal this one from you. It has always been about now, never later. The only way to anticipate a greater later is to ensure an undeniable now. If you only knew you were the before and afterlife, you wouldn't allow them to dictate either!

Why I Decided to Kill Myself Today

Time being the most precious jewel hidden inside the rocks of life, it is finally my time to say goodbye.

So as you hammer out what this truly means don't be sad for me.

For sadness is a curse spewed from the mouths of those who lack hope and thrive upon the failures of others.

But I for a long time now have been waiting for the perfect moment to leave.

And perfection being a wand that only the hands of God can yield this moment long awaited twirls and sways so effortlessly leaving thin streaks of tranquility on my soul.

This world will never see my face again.

For so long they have hated me with extreme personality.

They have devoted all of their time to wasting mine cheating me out of what's rightfully owed at birth.

But today I come to collect on a bounty most earned knocking on society's door with frightening pound and bolstering voice.

They will hear and feel me for the very first time like new life.

They will wallow in their sorrow for allowing me to leave.

They will blame one another for missing the signs and look feverishly for answers to questions that their tongues are too swollen to speak of.

I reek of consciousness and confidence to kill myself as I heal myself.

This is the only way.

And at my funeral the words they'll say won't resemble the words they've said because the words they've said are no longer alive but dead and have been that way for an eternity and a day but it is only today that I've decided to join them!

But I will die well.

I will die trying to excel.

The pursuit of perfection will be wearing a vale and my pride will walk this bride down a twisted isle paved with my suicide.

And in my death resides my life as I kill myself and take the arm of my wife as we become twice the life they meant for us to be.

Better to die today than tomorrow because tomorrow may be too late to try and follow your dreams.

My dreams are supported by golden beams too tall and slippery for me to climb atop without both hands firmly grabbing and pulling me to freedom.

They think their hands are holding me down but they're just holding a corpse that resembles who I could have been if I would have been discouraged by the humiliating names they growled or the persecution they piled upon my shoulders. So with outstretched arms I am more than happy to kill myself because he was never I and I was never he.

That was just an impostor, a fake, a replica of a replica of me.

The one that you had broken down wrist bound by old rusty chains of hurt and pain.

The one you slurred discouraging words and had tied up on the curbs and corners of your hoods then embarrassingly locked away behind bars never to see sunlight play hide and go seek with the children of clouds.

The one you allowed gunfire too loud to cloud the vision of a brilliant child who had to run, hide and cry underneath beds made by arms of hate.

That's who kissed my fiery forehead and cold tucked me in at night.

The one whose knees are scarred and hands are callused from kneeling down praying on shattered dreams and holding on to broken promises never to be mended.

This world intended to kill me.

But they failed because that was never me!

That was a fraud, a mod, a sloppy carbon copy, a clone, a mirage, an illusion to an illusion and misinterpretation of who I am.

I am that I am and if I am that I am then I am more than I am

and today I am going to show them that I am by washing their hands clean from the blood of killing me.

As I spiritually kill myself.

And in my death lies the true novelty of life.

For I could never become anew through old means, old dreams and unfortunate things.

So you can have the old me, the one you had gasping for air as you choked inspiration and mutilated motivation from his mind.

His time is no longer mine.

His mind you will no longer find captivated by your war against him.

Because time has fastened his coat and is reaching for the door.

So I will no longer ignore the promise I made this world that I would do more than just survive.

I promised to be alive.

And that's the reason why I have no choice but to kill myself, not just today but every single day!

When your nightmares are real they will truly haunt you and try to destroy your will to live. This is when in life it becomes vital for you to follow your dreams because within those dreams resides the courage of life!

From the Mind

What is Wisdom?

Wisdom is not knowledge. Wisdom is your ability to use knowledge, power and understanding to invoke a greater purpose. Everyone is born with common sense. Even animals have that. But wisdom is something that must be attained. It is sought out, not given. It is tracked down, not found. And to obtain true wisdom in life one must self evaluate with deep honesty and integrity first. So to be wise one must become wise. Be wise my friends! Be wise!

Stop Looking for Unicorns

The world continues to look for unicorns when it already has rhinos. Don't miss out on the big show watching the monkeys dance in front of the main stage. Appreciate that life is a slight of hand that will disappear right in front of your eyes and reappear wearing bells, whistles and a painted face with a big red nose and balloons to give away. But when the bells' dings go to dongs, whistles no longer whisk and balloons pop, all that's left is a concrete jungle that will either eat you alive or let you survive. It's your choice...always has been...always will be!

These Three B's of a Fulfilled Life

So **be diligent** about your life because you only get to be careful about it once. Your life is a priceless vase that should be held against your chest with two hands because dropping it would be truly tragic. **Be meticulous** with your thoughts because they precede your actions. What you think will always be so those thoughts are the foundation of your happiness. And last but not least **be tireless** in the moment. Take advantage of tenacity and seize every moment as if it were your last, because it certainly could very much be!

Deserve Nothing But Be Worth Everything

People who deserve much attain little, but those who are worth more obtain more. Be careful in which spirit you have. A deserving spirit tends to lie to itself making one believe that it is owed. But how can one be owed in an existence it has not chosen? Rather than believing in what you deserve, believe in what you are worth. A worthy spirit arrives only after the sacrifice has been made. And a worthy spirit receives what it is worth, which is usually much more than what it deserves.

Feed Your Soul's Flame

In life the word potential is often misused as a way to measure our abilities.
And it is also used to excuse the lack of progress of unsuccessful activity.
Do not feel special if you have potential because everyone's born with potential.
What separates typical from great is one's ambition.
Ambition is the small flame that ignites in the souls of people with potential.
These souls have an extreme need for greatness.
It is then the courage of ambitious souls that feeds the burning desires of greatness that ultimately allows ambition to overwhelm all doubts and adversities that normally hinder success.
Therefore to become great your ambition needs to be fueled by execution that allows your flame to explode and engulf the negative rhetoric and disbelief of all non believers!

Respect but Don't Accept the Struggle

Discipline is easier as topic of discussion than it is accomplished.
It is not until adverse moments that it should even be measured.
Growth is accompanied by pain.
Success is accompanied by failure.
And appreciation of these things is a rare but necessary trait to inevitably overcome all obstacles.
Respect the struggle, but don't accept it. Amen.

The Power of Belief and Consequences of Disbelief

It is not the assault of adversity tearing through your will to succeed that's shattering your dreams.

Nor the paralysis of poverty cementing the soles of your soul to stand steadfast in the rummage of self doubt and pity.

It is not the vile misdirected slurs slithering from treacherous tongues spewed from mouths of hate that sting your subconscious mind into desolate places.

Nor the ill advised plots of evil men drawn up in private halls and societies of secret that burden your back with insecurity and guilt, hindering your climb to greatness.

It is simply your disbelief in yourself and your misbelief in what it actually takes to become more that disables you.

So don't you think it's about time to believe?

Tame the Beast

Life indeed is a fickle beast.

And there will be defining moments in yours that no matter how you react, the instances will cause catastrophic differences in how the world moves for and around you.

But the key to a successful life is to at least have a reaction.

Giving up is not an option for the living.

And pity is a drug for the confused mind.

So never die until you're dead.

And tame the beast with all your heart and soul.

Because Life will always be a fickle beast, but your ability to react doesn't have to be!

Successful People View Life As An Opportunity, Not A Task

When looking at life see everything as an opportunity, not a task.

Tasks are things in life people dread to complete. Instead of seeing things as a task, see them more as an opportunity.

You have an opportunity to work, not a task to work.

You have an opportunity to serve, not a task to serve.

You have an opportunity to succeed, not a task to try to succeed.

In opportunity lies the ability to be impressive. In tasks there only lies the ability of completion.

In opportunity you can exploit greatness, uniqueness and worth.

In tasks the greatest exposure comes from failure.

Start turning all of your life's tasks into opportunities and watch success follow you everywhere just like your shadow!

Be Water to the Stone

Beware as the stones of disappointment are everywhere, but do not be afraid.
Be water when adversity blocks your path and just go around.
Seep through the ridicule.
Drown oppression.
Soak in knowledge.
And when the weight of the world is dropped on your shoulders disperse underneath, gather yourself together and keep flowing.
There is an ocean of opportunities and enlightenment awaiting your arrival and all you have to do to get there is empty into it!

Instead of trying to see if the grass is greener on the other side, know that it is simply because you had to ask. And then do something about it. Water your side with knowledge. Nurture your side with understanding. And then grow your side with sun rays of execution.

Success & Fear Are Not Friends

Fear is the equivalent of zero plus zero if you don't allow it to add up into something more by dividing your ambitions and eventually turning your mentality into something less. Subtract doubt from your inner self. Multiply your work ethic substantially. And realize that fear is accepted, not mandated!

To become great one must try to be great. There is nothing wrong with trying. There's only something wrong with presuming and calling it faith. Do not confuse faith with fear. They are not the same things. Trying precedes faith. But fear will allow one to proceed only to stagnancy. So be great and try at all cost. You have nothing to lose but yourself by not doing so!

Life Chose You, React Accordingly

Life is not dictated, it is accepted. You must accept that you have not chosen it but rather it has chosen you. And in that lies the challenge. Therefore you cannot challenge Life, but it can certainly challenge you. What is important in this challenge is letting Life know who you are, as that is what you can dictate. Are you someone that's easily defeated? Are you someone who easily bows down to the adversity that's already beneath you? Or are you the magnificent vessel that has awed this world time and time again? You cannot dictate Life. But you can truly dictate who Life is dealing with. And once Life knows who it is dealing with it reacts accordingly!

Two Lies

The most detrimental person to lie to in this life is yourself. Once you've crossed that line lying to others becomes common place. However, these two lies are not the same. They don't weigh the same. They don't resemble the same qualities. And they don't have the same consequences. When you lie to yourself it is normally more disguised, less subtle to you. But when you lie to others it's the exact opposite, as lying to others is strategically done. It is the unrecognizable lies to one's self that slowly but surely deteriorates your health and makes one look and feel older than necessary. The weight of lying to yourself should not be carried mentally or physically by you for any period of time. But excessively carrying lies to yourself for long periods of time will break you down unto death. You are strong, but none of us is that strong. So pass that burden to someone else. Let someone else act happy when they are not. Let someone else act fulfilled when they are not. But let yourself honor the truth and have enough courage to positively address what you already know. Your mind and body are begging you to do so before it's literally too late.

Cement Shoes of Disbelief

There's nothing in this world that can stop you from rising except the cement shoes of your own disbelief. You don't have to wear them at all. Free the feet of your mind and walk on top of your fears. Spread the wings of a creative imagination and fly above your anxiety. Elevate with the purpose of a mountainous wind and blow through the treacherous trees of doubt that drape in front of your soul's window. Hover above the distractions of mediocre men and lend no ear to the teachings of confused and wavering women. Your rise comes from a familiar place within, a place you have abandoned. Return back to the self you know and rise to the person you were always meant to be!

You Are a Book of Life

We as human beings need to acknowledge the pages of our perception.

We must be consciously aware of the narrative our book of life reads.

And the only way to honestly know how that narrative reads is by reflecting on what others perceive of us.

The story that we think our life is telling everyone is not always on the same page of what is truly being read.

We are all authors of our own legacy and there's excitement in that alone.

But we must remember that the lives we write everyday is being written not for us, but for them. And even though we already know our own story, it is others that may be confused when reading us.

So as human beings we must take responsibility for their confusion as we are the artist of our own life's book.

Therefore our stories are only as good as the reviews rendered.

And as writers we must indulge the needs of our audience if we truly care about those we interact with while the pages of our lives are still being turned.

Feed the Three

There are critical functions that make up your existence.
Three of them are your heart, your soul and your mind.
And they must all be fed for you to live, not survive.
Feed your heart by loving others more.
Your heart is hungry and will only be fed by the ones you show love to.
Feed your soul by persevering through your struggles.
Overcoming adversity is a nutrient that your soul cannot do without.
Feed your mind by being more creative.
Creativity allows your mind to swallow up confusion and challenges it to digest opportunities.
If you don't feed your heart, your soul and your mind you cannot grow.
If you're not growing, you're dying.
And if you're only trying to survive, you're not living.
So I encourage you to live.
And to do that you must feed!

Fear Is For The Unborn

Fear is not something you're born with.
It is gift wrapped in sheets of insecurity
and then personally delivered to you by self pity and self hatred.
But you are the only one that has the power to not accept these types of gifts.
Fear is free but will end up costing you so much more than belief.
Belief is priceless and fortunately something you're born with.
Don't gift wrap your belief in despair and give it up to anyone, ever.
Instead believe in yourself.
Believe in something bigger than you.
And believe that fear is for the unborn.

Love All Others First And True Happiness Will Follow

The true key to happiness lies in our ability to honestly love all people for their differences, realizing that they are us and we are them. We cannot honesty love ourselves until we honestly love one another. To reach this blissful reality we must bury our egos to resurrect our humanity, as we seek to understand each other before we demand understanding of ourselves. We are all merely ripples in a sea hope and splashes of all kind is what ultimately pushes everyone ashore.

Stay Humble

Many have lost. Many have cried. Many have died. And at any given time you could have been any of them, and in return they you. But in any case you cannot become gold being silver. And I say that to say this. Remember where you come from and that you deserve absolutely nothing in this life, but are worth absolutely everything.

Leadership is less of a choice and more of a destiny. We do not lead because we want to, but because we have to. For we are not willing to accept where the train ends up unless it is us who have laid the tracks!

A Rolling Stone Grows No Algae

It's not always good to keep jumping from one plain to another. Sometimes it's in your best interest to stay grounded. A rolling stone can grow no algae. So sometimes when you're confused you just need to be still, be silent and listen to the voice of your next move. If you listen close and long enough you'll sometimes hear patience telling you to be patient. You'll sometimes hear diligence whispering to you to be diligent. And in that obedience a new opportunity will present itself in the arms of your current situation. But also be rest assured that if algae does not present itself to you after you have turned away from rolling for what you know has been a considerable amount of time, it is well time for you to leap towards something new, different and worthwhile. In the end time is your most valuable possession and to irresponsibly lose it while jumping or grounding would simply be uncivilized.

Visions are coming to you with great ambition and determination. They have permission to do so from your mind. Your mind has sent a vision to you with a message of how to accomplish something that you truly want. if your vision becomes a dream that will only be because you just didn't listen to what your mind had to say. Listen today, it'll be well worth it!

Fruits of Life

Loyalty is not a fruit that falls from the tree. It is the tree that bares the fruits of friendship, brotherhood and sisterhood. These fruits are the tastes of humanity that allow us to swallow life without pause. If your loyalty is strong the fruit it bares will remain. Weak loyalty bares rotten fruit that ends up in the dirt where it belongs. Become loyal. Be Loyal. And most of all stay loyal.

Greatness waits for no one. So when it stops by your place you need to immediately get your effort onboard, because if you hesitate and turn around by the time you turn back greatness will be long gone!

Mirror Mirror off the Wall

Life is the mirror that reflects who we truly are at all times. Sometimes that mirror gets foggy from adversity steamed up by hardships and despair. But as a people our ambition, hopes and dreams are the towels and cloths waiting to be picked up by our own loving hands to wipe away spots and streaks that skew our view. And only then with honest eyes can we look at our lives and smile back at what is truly being reflected.

Many of you are looking for huge and enormous ways to impact humanity positively. But for the one major thing you're looking for if you would just do the many small things that you can easily do that present themselves to you on a regular basis moment by moment each day, these would outweigh the one thing you're looking for by tons and ultimately fill a void inside of you that only exist by the absence of your own hand.

There will be times throughout your life that you will get to build relationships with people that truly matter. These will be your true brothers and sisters in life. You will know them not by how many times they've been there for you in your time of need, but by how they know they can come to you in the midnight hour and your back would not be turned against them, regardless of their need. Your true friends still give you butterflies when you talk to them. Your true friends you are still cautious of what words you use around them because you value your friendship. You won't have to communicate with them often, but they know and you know that the connection you have is real, eternal and unbreakable. Your goal becomes to never intentionally hurt them and if you unintentionally do so you immediately apologize and ask for their forgiveness because it makes you sick to your stomach to disappoint them. Some of these connections take time and some of them don't. But all of them when they are real are less about how these people make you feel and more about how you have the eternal desire to make them happy. Because that ultimately makes you happy.

Respect and Loyalty

Respect & Loyalty are totally two completely different things. Do not mistake one for the other. Respect is a two way street that needs traffic both ways to ensure jams & collisions don't exist. However Loyalty is a one way hall that echoes loudly even when you tip toe. It doesn't travel both ways because it's not conditional. You will know all those who are disloyal when adversity is at your doorway and the halls are all quiet.

If You Don't We Will

Your heart is the greatest gift ever given.
So much so that possession of such a gift is impossible.
Therefore your heart is yours to build, but not to break.
Yours to pump, but not to bleed.
Yours to find, but not to lose.
For one cannot lose what one never had.
However, if summoned correctly your greatest gift
can become our greatest prize.
And ultimately we can then save the world, together.
One heart at a time,
if you don't love.
We will.

Your soul is the greatest gift ever given.
So much so that possession of such a gift is impossible.
Therefore your soul is yours to lift, but not to fly.
Yours to elevate, but not to drown.
Yours to save, but not to lose.
For one cannot lose what one never had.
However, if summoned correctly your greatest gift
can become our greatest prize.
And ultimately we can then save the world, together.
One soul at a time,
if you don't rise.
We will.

Your mind is the greatest gift ever given.
So much so that possession of such a gift is impossible.
Therefore your mind is yours to command, but not to have.
Yours to beseech, but not to own.
Yours to share, but not to lose.

For one cannot lose what one never had.
However, if summoned correctly your greatest gift
can become our greatest prize.
And ultimately we can then save the world, together.
One mind at a time,
if you don't mind.
We will.

Time is the only thing that we have and do not have all at once. It is the most valued possession on earth. Thank you for taking time to read

A Violin For Your Crow and experiencing this life with me. As I know your time is precious, sharing it with me is highly appreciated. I hope that you enjoyed A Violin For Your Crow as much as I enjoyed sharing it with you.

You can reach me at:
www.jessebensonbooks.com
jessewbensontheauthor@gmail.com
jwbenson23@gmail.com
@JBENzChronicles on Facebook